soundswrite 2015

Anthology of contemporary poetry

SOUNDSWRITE
PRESS

ISBN: 978-0-9550786-8-2

First published 2015 by
SOUNDSWRITE PRESS
52 Holmfield Road
Leicester LE2 1SA
Email: soundswrite@ntlworld.com
www.soundswritepress.co.uk

Cover image:
Driftwood Woman by Anne Fishenden

Printed and bound by Lightning Source UK Ltd

Orders:
Individual copies £5 (plus £1.50 UK p&p)

Typeset in Gills Sans MT & Times New Roman

Acknowledgements:

Thanks are due to the editors of the following magazines, where some of the poems first appeared: *Acumen*, *The Interpreter's House*, *Iota*, *Magma*, *The Rialto*.

As it usually does, *Shibboleth* and *There you go!* appeared in Common Ground by D A Prince (Happen*Stance* Press, 2014); *Clothes horse*, *Suave and debonair* and *Flown* appeared in Beyond the Tune by Jayne Stanton (Soundswrite Press, 2014). *Greig Street* by Bernice Read appeared in Things You Ought to Know (Derby City Poets, 2013).

CONTENTS

INTRODUCTION

Soundswrite was formed in 2000 as a group open to all women who share an enthusiasm for poetry. It has met regularly since then, usually twice a month, in Leicester. Membership has expanded over time; of the twelve poets who appeared in our first anthology (2005) seven are represented in this, our fourth anthology, which contains work from seventeen poets. These anthologies do not follow a regular calendar but appear when we feel the group is ready.

Fifteen years on from our first meeting, this anthology consists of poems from women who have been regular members of the group during 2014. Each poet submitted six poems. Our task as editors was to select the poems which contributed most to make the anthology cohesive and representative of the group at its best. We were looking for a dialogue between the poems, for poems that engaged and supported each other; we had no fixed ideas of theme or structure but simply looked to see what would emerge as current concerns. We regarded all poems as equals, whether or not they had been published before. Some excellent poems had to be excluded simply because they did not sit easily next to others in the anthology. We believe these 53 poems join together to reflect the range and outward-looking ethos of Soundswrite. We hope you enjoy them as much as we enjoyed working with them.

Davina Prince & Marilyn Ricci, Leicester 2015.

CHRISTINE COLEMAN

Light harvest

October is the time to harvest light,
on days when lingering strands of summer
drift into a sky that rings like glass,
honing the dulled edges of your sight
to gather all the shift and shimmer
of slanting sun on trees and tawny grass,
touching the familiar with surprise.

This morning I escaped into a park
where light lay ripe and waiting for my eyes,
trapped on wet black mud – splintering on dark
green spikes of holly into shards so bright
I'll feast all winter on this hoard of light.

CAROLINE COOK

Keats in autumn

Season of misseds and mellows, browns and yellows, ooze
and snags of brambles, stubble, sickle, swath and gourd,
of kissed and unkissed, gathered in, cast off, of wind
falls, leaf-fall, leaves and leavings, winnowing and fire.
Remember him! who ripened marvellously young,
who saw small number of your live performances,
but felt in full the steady robbery of light.

D A PRINCE

As it usually does

the wind gets up about this time
sneaky with just enough tug
flicking a page or loose hair
or somebody else's sweet wrapper
tipping over shingle and stone
and half-hearted patches of sand
children claim for storybook seaside
sandcastle business
the moat always leaking and the youngest
tottering with excitement egged on
by *careful!* and *watch it!*
the tide going out or coming in
appearing to do neither

and the question's there like a cloud
miles out to sea and small
only a scrap in the sky but it'll grow
when we have to give something sorry
to its goosebumped nagging
won't take no
insists until it's covering the whole sky
and *where did that come from?*
newspapers flapping like flags
picnics shredded, even the gulls
pitched off the rooftops and now
the weather's really coming rough
dragging the horizon.

ELIZABETH HOURSTON

The road to Hermaness

Do you know the road to Hermaness

where the land meets the sea
and the sea meets the sky

where the wind sucks the breath
out of you and scours your bones

where salt reddens your eyeballs
and stings bitter on your tongue?

Leave behind the houses and fields
and man-made dykes and follow

the unmarked track until you come
to the wild sea and raging sky

where dishevelled feathers flutter
and ravening bonxies dive

where the light is white and hard
and the colours true.

Elizabeth Hourston

Between weathers

We are at sea.

        Astern, cloud and mist
lour low on Thurso Bay.

        Sudden sun
scorches the cliffs of Hoy to embered red.

A sough of wind, fickle as history,
funnels through Rackwick and falls still.
Ahead, the Kame is lost in fretted haar.

A yellowed gannet hangs beside the *Hamnavoe,*
poised

        and I turn again to you.

KATE RUSE

Night fishing

One night when I was small
the amah with the soft voice
wrapped me up in a shawl of feathers
and took me down to the brim of the lake
where her lover's eyes skimmed the water
in the crackling fire light.
At times the flames seemed to cry out
it's just the wind heaving in the branches
the amah said, beneath her coat her best
cheongsam, the one with the blue satin brocade,
tightened round her nakedness.
We scurried past the creaking rafts
sometimes a wail grew then faded
followed by the wheeze and hiss of wood
shrinking and blackening in the heat.
The amah's heart was caught in her lover's net
she stood shivering pulling the sodden coat around her
while he moved swiftly in the smoke
tying the snare round the cormorant's throat.

Lizzie Madder

Mermaid in the cove

I see you, head above the waves,
a spectre of silver, shimmering

in a sea of jade and turquoise
sparkling with diamonds.

I hear your cry, a haunting distress
of anguish and suffering.

The grief of a woman in despair
her child lost forever, her man has gone.

Queen of the Seals: I cannot rescue you,
you must stay and swim with your sisters.

One day, a fisherman discovering you in his nets
may free you from your curse.

How will you measure your freedom
when you walk on the shore, look out to sea?

CHRISTINE COLEMAN

The dress

She lets herself be funnelled
into the mould, the jewelled
bodice with its knotted lacing
under the teeth of the zip
and the tight row of buttons
all down the length
of her spine.

The rendering of ivory silk
has been designed to draw the eye,
caress the curves, then fall away
in shining streams to sweep
the aisle, control her pace,
inhibit any backward step
and hem her in.

The bridesmaids and the mother
know the dual functions of the dress –
they've scrutinised the structure
of the underskirt, examined every
nook and cranny of the satin cave
with all its layered
frippery of net.

They know the fishtail form was her
own choice, but now it almost seems
the dress chose her. After the feast
they'll hoist the fabric up to let
her dance – in spite of their
uneasy dreams of
mermaids' feet.

Fur

She wore a black velvet choker around her throat,
and a chatelaine at her waist for her watch –
silver, good quality – which hung with her scissors
and the key to her mahogany chest.
Every day she unlocked the top drawer
to stroke the fox tippet she kept for best.
She put a bit by each week, slipping the coins
into a glove tucked under her nightdress,
to save for the chinchilla she'd seen in Leah's.
She bought vegetables from the market
late in the day, and it was cheaper
to skin a rabbit herself than to ask the butcher.
With plenty of bread, she'd make it last two dinners
as she pictured herself in full length fur.

CHRISTINE COLEMAN

When I can choose

I'll live in a house with high ceilings,
and practise topiary.

Yew hedges will take root
along the skirting boards.

I'll clip them into crenellations
below the roses on the coving,

gouge out small, square windows
to let green light spill in.

New fronds, bright as limes
will stroke my cheek, my palms,

and winter berries will kindle
the white tips of my fingers.

I'll curl up on the springy floor
of camomile and thyme. Trace

familiar features in the dark.
Wind will stream up from the river,

clatter through the aspen leaves.
Drown out the one not chosen.

MICHELE BENN

Greek myth

Three Greek women
in widows' weeds
waddle downhill
in the skin-scorching
heat of the morning sun.

Black dresses constrict
big round bellies.
Bandy legs end in sturdy sandalled
flat feet slapping the dirt-track
sending clouds of dust
up from the baked earth.

On reaching the shore
three bright apple-bodies emerge
wrapped in floral swimsuits
sturdy arms and strong suntanned legs
striding over stones
stepping into the crystalline sea
bobbing like buoys
their inflated laughter
drowning out the drilling drone
of invisible cicadas.

Whilst in the village
on top of the hill
living Greek husbands
hang freshly-washed underpants
on lines strung out under
vine-covered canopies.

KATE RUSE

Lotus

she slips from shadow corners to sunlit rooms
her parents' kisses still warm on her cheeks
but she has a long way to go before she meets him
the whole length of the house

in the hallway the perfume of jasmine drifts
wild orchids with frills and forked tongues hang
from the verandah   she smooths her gown   then her hair
in another room the tea sits cooling

will he expect her to dance on her lotus feet
already lame she falters   in an ante room
a bird hops from perch to perch
rings a bell   cocks its head at her

D A PRINCE

There you go!

Here you are with your life dangling
plastic over a 2 for £5 tee-shirt,
ID flashing a chubby photo grinning
when your hair was darker and
there wasn't only fifteen minutes left on your break,
checkout fumbling each bar code,
everyone paying by card, system
struggling, the month too long for the money,
a Tannoy begging Mr Jones to come to the phone,
somebody's split pack leaking sugar,
forgetting to bring a bag again,
settling for the own brands, the Value,
the Everyday, what they'll eat without fussing,
and the same lopsided sign-off.

Here you are telling Lisa, later, lighting up
by bins over-bulged with black plastic,
freed from your screens, spinning out Marlboroughs,
laughing where you'd like to be, given the chance
or Lottery, always the same unlucky numbers,
photos winking at each other, when she cuts in
No and *They don't call it Tannoy no more*,
so that's one more fuck-up, owed
to your mam's scrapbook phrases, the ones you'd scoffed at –
return half of a ticket, shillings for the gas,
how the doctor knows best, suffer in silence,
take a Rainmate just in case,
when it was *Mind how you go!* and a peck,
always making the best of a bad job.

BERNICE READ

Plot lines

No gardens in Brick Lane;
and Grandfather Davies, by all accounts,
too sozzled – or he could have been restricted
by his rooted preoccupation
with those *Stones of Venice.*

So when did the earthiness enter?
Was it one cat-loving grandmother
still sad for a Minsk beetroot patch
or the other for her Connemara outback?
Or was it that yellow-clay clag
at the edge of a rickety steel town
where a Dig-for-Victory groundbreak
grew on for a Jew-boy's roses?

He can't have been a gardener
said my great aunt Rachel.
Not true: and through one of those conduits
a little green has trickled, marked my fingers.

Maxine Linnell

Threads

A summer spent hunting the best price
for panama hat, beret, shirts, tie,
skirt hung on the knee, navy knickers,
long white socks, sensible shoes.

The name tapes live at the bottom
of the sewing box. With glasses and thimble,
you sew tapes on netball shirt, hockey shorts.
They smell of not knowing the rules.
They are too white to hide behind.

Today I sit with you sewing your name
on underwear thin with washing.
You say this new home
is like the boarding school you longed for,
but not quite.

The needle pierces skin.
I cut the thread
with my teeth.

KAREN POWELL

Signet ring

Stacked on his workbench with boxes of nails,
an army ration tin. Forcing open
the warped lid, she sifts through francs, guilders,
shrapnel, marks and eagle insignia.
She hands me a silver crucifix –
not his, he wasn't religious.
Finds a gold signet ring, not engraved,
tries every finger to find the best fit.
She forgets he never wore jewellery.
No wedding ring, only a simple watch
with an expanding strap. Like the arm bands
that kept his sleeves at just the right length.
Heavy on eighty-year-old fingers,
she wears it always to keep him close.

HELEN JAYNE GUNN

Air waves

What was it drove me one night to put my dead mother's name
into Google? She, whose idea of hi-tech had been a cordless phone.
Internet heaven delivered a memorial page created
by God-knows-who or -what, with seventy-five hits.
Now seventy-six.
The tribute font was crisply cursive, compared to which her chatty
correspondence knocked out on a series of Imperial typewriters
seemed quaint as messages pressed in tablets of wet clay.
I had once badgered her to take seriously the wafer of my Nokia
whose predictive text she refused to trust long enough for hocus-pocus
letters to complete their quadrille. Her youth had been moulded by
                                                              analogues –
dreaded telegrams delivering only bad news; signals suggested a person
waving two flags through semaphore. Even wireless,
meaning those stout wooden boxes of her world war generation,
had been a bridge too far. The way voices came at you,
she'd once explained, close to fright, how they followed you
around   out of nowhere

MARILYN RICCI

What you left behind

Trainers with the shape of your bunions,
seeds for root veg, brassicas and onions,
a slim egg timer with small blue grains,
a broken brolly for inevitable rain,
a silver locket with tiny blurred faces,
six cotton hankies, two pairs of laces,
the keys to the house and garden shed,
the abridged Jane Eyre next to your bed,
a Sinclair computer and a floppy disc,
bus pass photo like a terrorist,
several cheap crossword books,
the proverbial trio of flying ducks,
three wooden spoons and a mixing bowl,
Unforgettable by Nat King Cole.

BERNICE REYNOLDS

Before the bathroom

A crochet-clothed table
set with best china cups,
crimped plates and saucers
near a roaring fire,
glistening guard.

Tin bath on red rag-rugs,
soft Welsh water
from enamel jugs
lathers soap lavishly,
steams silently.

Mother flannels
child's hands and feet,
blows soapy bubbles
before after-chapel family
arrive for supper.

Much amusement,
claps and cheers as
wet hair is wound into
elephant trunks, fairy wings,
fantasy creatures.

Dry and dressed,
her milky supper
is consumed along with
sermon recalls,
deep political debate

while wiry Deacon uncle's
paper-bagged *News of the World*
waits on the hall table
to be savoured along with
Monday's bacon breakfast.

CAROLINE COOK

In praise of deliquescence

Some say glass moves
– that it is only waiting
in suspense for a return
to a once looser state,
and who could blame it?

Some say that in the Stone Age
desert nomads fashioned blades
out of dark clumps where sizzling ash
had bombed on sand.

Enter Obsidian and Tektites

Old Pliny tells us,
as the Syrian sun set,
a Phoenician boat, a bireme,
put in off the shore near Sidon,
and its oarsmen, eager for a meal,
rushed out with cauldrons,
but they found no rocks to lay them on.
Loud were their curses!
Thus they hauled out of the cargo
blocks of nitrate, placed these on the beach
and lit their fires beneath their pots.
Then, Baal be praised!
soft sand and nitrate mingled.   Streams
of an amazing liquid flowed: Al-kimiya of bonding!
It is said this recipe was etched
in supple clay.

Some say that if you had a cup
made out of stone and left it undisturbed
– if you put pieces of smashed glass
inside the cup and left them there,
you could return in, say, a million years
and find the glass relaxed,
turning to slush.

When we can travel in a time-machine,
some say we'll watch glass ooze like syrup.

I like syrup,
deep unclottings,
unset sunsets,
bending rulers,
loosening states.

BERNICE REYNOLDS

Waiting at the Oddfellows

They were always there, sitting on a bench
outside the Oddfellows Hall after lunch –
or as they referred to it – dinner time.
Dad-cu and I would tap our way along –
he with his walking stick and me with mine –
an old umbrella handle cut to size.

I have something to say about the size.
Fifty years later on an attic bench
I found the tiny stick which had been mine.
Took it downstairs and brought it out at lunch
just to show the girls who'd both come along
for a birthday meal celebrating time

with us. And I told them about the time
I was still a small child, about this size,
when Dad-cu would say *Sticks out! Come along!*
So we'd stride majestically to the bench
to confer with the Comrades after lunch.
They never would believe the stick was mine.

They don't send young gels like you down the mine
to be injured. They teased me every time.
I'm a girl, not a gel and you should say lunch
not dinner and the stick is just my size
so I can walk with Dad-cu to the bench.
And you know I'm not injured all along!

They'd budge up. I'd sit and listen along
with them to tales of ships, steel works, the mine
and how they'd been brought up before the Bench
for Refusing Active Service. Each time
I listened they grew in stature and size.
They'd worked, had dinners not lunch

to fuel their energies. They'd scoff at lunch
these wiry intense men who'd sang along
to pits or blazing furnaces the size
of Hell's hobs. They'd worked an intricate mine
which robbed them of breath and cut short their time.
They'd stayed comrades and remembered on the bench.

And I remember too. No son of mine
will toil underground or burn before time
to sit reminiscing on the Oddfellows bench

BERNICE REYNOLDS

In step

Snapped, all holding hands
they passed the Pavilion
walking along the Promenade
Daddy by the sea wall
Mam swinging a cloth bag
keeping their child safely centred

a passer-by glances their way
smiling slightly at the child's
deep concentration

noticing her trying
desperately
to keep in step
not to tread on the cracks
in the pavement.

Maxine Linnell

For drier times

The rain's slipped into mizzle,
mist, shades of wet air.
The wind's up, the river's mad, muddy swirls
catch on a stone, a rusting shopping trolley.

We tramp under the bridge,
trying our voices for the boom,
open the gate, flounder through mud,
stamp in puddles. You pick a leaf
off your shining yellow wellies, carefully,
then check your hands for dirt,
rub them together.

We stride the bumpy meadow, hoping for ducks
and woodpeckers, maybe a kingfisher.
Two dripping horses in dirty coats
under leafless trees let you stroke their noses.
We climb the rise like Everest.

Your hand's in mine. You hold my cracked life
light in your small palm. I hug you
right through your wet coat.

KATE RUSE

Smile

and there they are two black and white figures
leaning on each other   the way lovers do
behind them snow slips off boulevard trees
jazz drifts up from the flat below
they laugh at a wisecrack
after all the flag waving   redrawing of boundaries
reassembling what was lost by layers of war
I could freeze them   her eyes squinting at the low sun
or rip them apart   send him back to his child bride
to the California heat   send her
off to the backstreet knife
in a German town to the north
he lied   she believed an old story
played out again and again
leaving infants mangled by their mother's grief
leaving children thirsting for something unknown
so it is best to put down the picture
while they are still smiling   in monochrome

JAYNE STANTON

Clothes horse

On winter nights, this wooden workhorse stole our heat,
its frame spread wide to shoulder the line-dried failures.
Our double-bar electric fire purloined, it coaxed the steam
from dampened spirits, raised our hopes of extra layers.

On summer days, we pitched its A-frame on the back lawn,
lazed in army blanket shade, picnicked in coarse comfort –
a seersucker cloth, requisitioned milk & wafer biscuits served
from doll-sized plastic ware. Teacup pinky fingers raised,
we made small talk. Our stiff-limbed charges cooled,
skinny-dipped in a makeshift washing-up bowl pool.

BERNICE READ

The aunt's tale

Our mother's crony – there to side with her
in sister-squabbles that at times were venomous.
The one there always, beside each of us,
years later, for those funerals or tragedies.
Who sang – elusive snatches –
... *strolling one day down the* something *Arcade,*
Oh, oh, Antonio or even *All the nice girls ...*

She never married: my father said
she was too lazy – for no-one doubted
that she, of all of them, *had had her chances.*
Smoked – chain-smoked – *Passing Clouds,*
from slick-pink packages, a further irritant
for my father; and, again, in her fifties,
I see her back from the tobacconist's
to laugh at yet another proposal.

Blue-eyed, fair, fat. Imperturbable.
Died in Ryde, of a stroke, at seventy.

Those shreds of song –
... *left me alone-y-o ...*

as lovers recede into night.

ANNA CHEETHAM

Cut out – Henri Matisse

With large scissors Matisse cut paper,
using a lifetime's skill he shaped
a curve depicting both flesh
and muscle, implying bone
beneath would articulate the movement.
One leaping woman *Blue Nude*
with Green Stockings, made in a year
when I was young and leaping.

His shapes were stuck to painted paper,
or sometimes were merely pinned
where he needed them.
The pinning done by beautiful
young women.
Ah, beautiful women,
supporting this crippled,
old male genius.

No longer young, I occasionally
still leap; make installations, collages,
paint. All squeezed between
domestic and political demands.
When I need help to position,
hang, carry and pin,
oh where, oh where,
are the beautiful young men!

Helen Jayne Gunn

August at dance camp

I'm not in Ibiza and I'm not in Magaluf, I'm not in Croatia, or hot
                                                                    Cameroon
I'm in an Oxford field in a marquee, doing salsa with you.
There are puddles in my tent and earwigs in my wellies, there's straw
in my sleeping bag and a pile of dirty knickers, but who thinks laundretto
when I can flamenco with you. The food I bought at Asda
rotted limp in the heat and butter in the chill pack has oozed to defeat
but who wants gourmet, if I can bourrée with you? I've learned to tap
and lindy hop and watched Egyptian dance, I've whirled like a dervish
and spun into a trance. I've sweated like a pig because it's ten days on
                                                                    your feet
no bath, no fridge and not a squawk of telly – but who wants *Newsnight*
when I can cruise the night with you – and dubstep, body pop, boogie,
                                                                    stomp
and swing, dress steam punk or space man or be just me
camp-bedraggled and crumpled, dancing till dawn with you.

So who needs Beijing, Berlin or Peru? Let's tango
beneath this starry sky in an Oxford field – me and you.

KAREN POWELL

Heacham Beach

Ribbons of birds trail across the pewter sky
towards a lone horse-rider cantering
along the sea-flecked beach. A seagull climbs high,
back-winging, drops a plump blue-black mussel,
swoops to retrieve, repeats again, again, again.

I turn my eyes downwards, scan through
scatterings of red seaweed tangled
with crab exoskeletons picked clean.
I search for the one pebble or shell
to anchor this moment in my bones.

CLAIRE WINTRAM

Places I would rather not be include McDonalds:

except in Beijing,
    because of the promise of almost odour-free cubicled sit-down toilets

except in Warsaw,
    where, early on a snowbound Catholic Sunday, nowhere else
                                      was open,

except in Rzeszow,
    with the Polish Pope built in stone guarding the street corner as we
        struggled with sleeplessness from Stalinist beds,

except in Slough,
    the day I thought nothing more could go wrong, love being skittish,
                              but the car broke down

except in Manhattan,
    where my excuse was, my friend was in charge.

Karin Koller

Inbox

> *Darling Karin*
> *Happy birthday for 5/10*
> *Hope it was such a happy day for you.*
> *Much love to you beautiful friend*
> *Pammy xxxxxxxxxx*

I've never been called Darling in my life,
or celebrated my March birthday
in October, or had a friend called
Pammy. But, among many less so,
October 5th was indeed a happy day
and I'm grateful to this random act
of generous and human error.

D A PRINCE

The Russian doll's imaginary friend

Solid and smallest, all this family
packed round, where can she play? No wriggle-gap
or shrug-space; locked in a treasury of women
she breathes along cracks, tasting for sunlight
where the restless splinter of herself
might go, unwrapped and birch-y. Blinking.

Blonde (blonde sounds free), unsmiling, apronless.
Two long legs, a runner, staying out
drinking the white nights, faster than the Neva,
clever with wolf-speak, sending their howls
echoing to call down stars blistered
with travel. And not a painted flower on him.

BERNICE READ

Greig Street

... of the clunky pavements,
assorted, mongrel terraces.
The corner church that's squat
and homely in its warm sandstone,
a narrow car-track
apart from the glinted darkness
or shallows of the Ness River,
the metallic art-work
that's a footbridge
from the Rose Street Foundry.

All, every, day there is this clattering
of little wheels – the trolleys,
suitcases, pushchairs,
their song for the Bed and Breakfasts,
the Chinese Chippy and the Lease Expired,
the guilty smokers at their open windows –
a rhythm, to and from the noisy ring road.
All night long the happy diners
trailing homeward from the waterfront.
And, four a.m., a Yellow Submarine.

Tracing

The lines are squiggly around Donegal
so my pencil goes slow as I follow the coast
past Dunkineely, St John's Point and on to Killybegs.

Philip O'Riley wanders, peering into inkwells,
half-listening to others bright and beautiful in the hall,
leaving us Catholics alone.

The cliffs of Slieve League are no easier, a tiny tear,
the point squeaks, takes forever to reach past
Belfast and down to the Mountains of Mourne,

then to Dublin and finally Dun Laoghaire.
Philip comes close, leans over: *Teacher's Pet*;
while from the hall I hear all things are wise and wonderful,

which somehow reminds me of Saturday night with uncle Mick
and aunty Mary making a holy show, bawling out the songs
in the Emerald Club, though they wouldn't go back, not now.

MICHELE BENN

Shopping in Kidderminster

When her feet grow so cold
she can no longer feel her toes
she swaps her silk-scarf
for a grey 'baklava' helmet
and goes shopping for shoes
in 'Kiddiminster.'

Hairspray long-dissolved
in the salty sea-wind,
nail-polish chipped, flaking
she slips out of her fine leather sandals
and into old socks proffered
for *reasons of hygiene.*

She's given a pair of boots:
black faux-suede with zip-up sides
and no heel to speak of but
Plenty of room round the ankle
for thick woollen stockings.

At the till
the shopkeeper shakes her head
looks away.
You don't need to pay.

Helen Jayne Gunn

Arte Povera

I used to be a sculptor, constructing from cardboard.
Then I switched to Performance Art – began eating the stuff.
Some people think it's easy, earning coin ripping into cardboard

like it's pizza. They don't realise
the training involved. It takes dedication to turn homeless
cardboard shivering in fast food doorways into philosophy.

When I ate cardboard outside Harvey Nick's
cops chivvied me off to Poundland backstreets where to be honest
no one has energy for art unless it's aerosol protest shat over walls.

So I was forced into gallery gigs.
Curators, critics, launches – that tiny, boutique world –
but existential questions shrank my guts to an ulcerated knot.

So it was back to the streets.
My latest work involves insulation. Cardboard is still my thing –
stuffed up my jeans, my sleeves, packed tight under my coat.

When I stretch on a park bench
for a night of stargazing I could be the fat effigy
of some once-great king. When I walk I creak like trees.

BERNICE READ

A family

Whitechapel: Jews on the run.
Then twenty-year tensions touch off
a new diaspora from an old rabbi's
intransigence, as he sweats in Brick Lane,
to chisel out bread for clever sons
who want to swim in all that honey.

In the end, he leaves the old woman,
who has struggled with the language,
tracked down local schools,
despised her neighbours.
The children marry out, a few of them
silent till death about Jewish roots

and everyone quarrels and holds back
support from the ever-living parents.

This is not a pretty story.
Nowadays, they all try harder,
attend uncustomary weddings,
dance at discos, kiss
the pretty little no-faith brides,
without a thought of Jehovah.

And they take to their hearts, Ysabelle.
Her parents may never marry
but she'll be christened, respectably
decked out in a loose-frilled heirloom.
Whatever culture spells her name like that?
But they won't argue.
She has black hair and blue eyes
and enough has happened.

D A PRINCE

Shibboleth

Only a hairline. Nothing, they said.
It doesn't matter.
There's nothing to say.

Perhaps it's nothing. Only a small crack
no deeper than surface.
Nothing to talk about.

Does it matter? Smooth it over.
Nothing will show.
Don't look at it now.

We can ignore it, can't we.
Can't we ignore it?
In some lights it's invisible.

It's barely visible.
And if it's no deeper ...
Why can't we talk about something else?

Do we have to look at it?
It looks the same, doesn't it?
Doesn't it look the same?

I can't see why it matters.
Is it anything?
What is there to say?

It's just one of those things.
No one seems to know
how long this has been going on.

How long *has* this been going on?

CHRISTINE COLEMAN

Something like a stone

If I'd been asked a little while ago
what sadness is, and where it tends to grow,
I might have said: *it flourishes in shade*
of sombre yews, or sighs in swaying reeds
along black creeks that web a lonely marsh
or overflows from reservoirs of grief.

I'd not have said: *sadness unfolds like wings*
that must not fly too near the scorching sun.
I'd not have said: *sadness can weave a net*
to trawl more fine and rare discoveries.
I'd not have said: *sadness becomes a lens*
that focuses the edge of happiness.

I'd still not say, because I still don't know
if sadness is the kernel or the shell
for every nut of truth. I only know
that in my breast lies something like a stone
that was not there a little while ago.

Maxine Linnell

Weeds

The white, pink and that primrose yellow in the drawer
look tawdry now. The stiff black dress
is new. The fabric chafes, sweats at my body,
shuts me indoors to cool. Under the trees they rattle teacups,
smile at little things. I watch, half-hidden in curtains
smelling of dust, remember sitting out there
with you, breathing you in. The sun's too bright.
There's only what is lost. I turn away.

Weeks. The cloth softens with washing,
fits now. Winter suits black, chills its shape.
This morning the hem is unstitched again
from those long dusk walks in the woods.
Mending, the needle brights through,
black thread follows it, stands out.
The fabric bleaches, dye leaching away.

Months. Skin wears the collar,
long sleeves thin and fray.
Trees loosen their leaves.
I almost long to join the rest at tea,
find white lace scraps to craft a collar,
cuffs, and try them. Look in the swing mirror
at that stranger face, white-framed,
the lace cuff as I touch new lines, the sunken mouth.
Fold the pieces in a drawer. Pick up my book.

Perhaps one day, a pale jewel at the throat.
A few months on, that bright blue shawl.
A year or two, the lilac blouse he liked so much –
the colour brought out my eyes, he said,
smiled right at me, dazzling, reached out to smooth
a curl strayed on my cheek. His finger brushed
my mouth. I almost feel it now.

50

MAXINE LINNELL

Beeman

Shading our eyes, we see the bees.
They drift around a corner of the roof,
hover, drop to flowers for supplies
and glide back up. They could be stinging now.

The beeman brings binoculars.
Bumblebees. The May full moon's
enticed them here to play and mate
among the gutters. A gift, he says,
they've come to show you there's a crack
in a tile or somewhere in the soffits.

The queen's taking her pick.
Bee testosterone sends them wild.
It won't last long, he says.
They're gone by June, the nest too.
They'll do no harm up there.

Standing by him, I see the gift of bees,
appreciate their dance, their crumbling nest.
Wild bumblebees chasing the moon.

MARILYN RICCI

On Rotherslade Beach

He hauls himself to the next level.
Those rocks are slippery, watch your footing,
her voice carries across the sands.

He waves an arm, not looking back,
grips the rock above with both hands,
hauls himself to the next level.

The sea insists against the rocks,
she sits down, shades her eyes,
her voice carries across the sands:

That's far enough, you're climbing too high,
allows glittering sand to flow through her fingers.
He hauls himself to the next level.

The sea crashes in, sucks back.
How does the world look from there?
Her voice carries across the sands.

He tightropes across a jagged mountain range,
picking his way from the sea, the land, then
hauls himself to the next level.
Her voice carries across the sands.

Claire Wintram

For Alex

You've left home now.
The fridge fills up with cherry yogurt
and no friends call.
The phone lies wreathed in silence,
no smiling mates at the door,
no crumbling mud on the stairs.
No smooth melodies, eliding into one,
floating through the air from the strings of your beloved guitar.
The washing line hangs empty,
the radiator grieves for its festoon of greying socks.
No shower tray filled with hair,
no bristles in the sink.
No taramasalata
and much less laughter.
I am left, eating up a freezerful of bagels.

JAYNE STANTON

Suave and debonair

your wisecrack
on the hallway mirror's viewpoint.

Brylcreem-slick, that wayward quiff
has aspirations – think Rock Hudson, Tony Curtis.
Weathered jaw line, razor-tame, *Old Spiced.*
Laundered shirt, worn
open-necked with the signature cravat,
always paisley, burgundy on gold.

Daddy's girl, my angle's blind
to a thinning crown, the comb-over;
a weak heart under peacock swagger – and
you're taller, somehow, out of overalls
in slacks with knife-edge creases down
to spit and polish; hands in pockets
weighing small change possibilities.
You shrug your shoulders
into a houndstooth blazer, square
the broken checks of green and cream;
leather buttons left undone, token casual.

My formative years in toughened hands:
our lifelines grafted, till you learn the art of letting go.

JAYNE STANTON

Flown

Jukebox pumped for hits, I plump for oldies,
inhale the bar fug, wheedle seats for two;
take in the sepia stains on anaglypta walls that reek
of *Snug* and *Ladies' Lounge* and matriarchs in hairnets
eking out their milk stout halves behind etched screens.

Elbows on the glass-ringed counter, proud,
you claim your patch, avoid the spilt beer; light up
an uncensored cigarette, relish its nicotine rush.
Order cola, a pint of Best and a whisky chaser.
Easy company: the daughter on a flying visit, father
plied with refills till he's whisky-winged.

Oiled, you sing On the Street Where You Live
for all the world as if you're Vic Damone,
I have often walked on this street before
but the pavement always stayed beneath my feet before.

Heading south, I tune to pirate radio, drown out
all that stereo babble from the fledged nest.

KARIN KOLLER

Baptism

Granny One is Catholic and will ensure
the well-being of her soul.

Granny Two is atheist and will ensure
she learns to swim.

JAYNE STANTON

Ritual

No silver spoon, Grandma Connelly dispenses
with a practised eye; upends a quarter pound of loose leaf,
stokes the teapot's fire-cracked belly, silences the kettle,
scalds the dried black heap, then stirs.

Her tincture eddies, adds a further burnt sienna lining
to the elephantine Betty. Left to mash in a hand-knit cosy,
brown spout raised, this worker signs our Sunday afternoon
in paisley swirls of aromatic steam

then genuflects to each in turn as Grandma pours
her benediction on the mismatched china. I serve
the bottled milk and sugar cubes, take up the offertory
in tea cards – my Brooke Bonds.

Super Strength, this stand-your-spoon-up-in-it brew
has muscles; *vulgari-tea*, my mother calls it. Still, we sip
its tannin, bitter through the Tate & Lyle scree.
I swallow my displeasure at the unstrained leaves.

Tea cups drained, returned to their saucers, Grandma swoops,
swills the dregs, reserves the residue, peers
into our far futures. As she ruminates
I wonder when she'll teach me housewives' runes.

Elizabeth Hourston

Grandmother

Half-smiling, she squints into the sun,
looks straight at me, unseeing.
And I stare back at her, devouring
the droop of her eyelids, her nose, the lines
around her mouth and eyes that show
how she has laughed and cried.

I see her hair, parted
in the middle, drawn softly back
behind her neck; study her hands
loose by her side, fingering
her skirt. I see the door behind her,
partly open, flowers sprouting by the wall.

And I grieve for her because she
never knew her son would have
a wife; never knew that wife
would have a child, who, one day,
would look at the image of a woman
she never knew, searching for a
likeness.

MICHELE BENN

Yahrzeit

last night
the yahrzeit light
burnt a hole
through memory
to a candle left unattended
that fasting Kol Nidrei evening
returning from our
Prayers of Repentance
to a smoke-cloaked room
a scorching hole
in the old oak table
near the candlewick-covered bed
left undisturbed
until this burning anniversary
of her death

walls stripped bare
pasted with white-washed anaglypta
a new Hygena dining table
four matching chairs
for our shrunken family
of three
and one sitting empty
in the space
where Nona's warm bed
once stood

ANNA CHEETHAM

Doctor's appointment

So, she said, *a twenty three*
point eight percent chance
of having a stroke
in the next ten years.
Well I'd be eighty six,
not too bad then,
but *stroke* doesn't mean *dead*,
in the could be *tomorrow*.
Would I want *tomorrow*?
Would I want
unable to speak,
difficult to walk?
On the other hand what would
I want?

Best I think is to
swim strongly out to sea
and keep going.
Just keep going.

Must remember to get
to the sea while I can
still swim and before
I forget
why I'm
going.

Lizzie Madder

Burne Jones windows
Harris Manchester Chapel, Oxford

Whether you believe or not,
to turn the stories into
those glorious technicolour windows
is a miracle of its own.

Here, angels solemnly gaze
through prisms of light
and the heart shreds
into a thousand shards of colour.

Karin Koller

Admission

With a certain reluctance I admit
sometimes I see you busying yourself
in a place I find myself calling: *up there*.

It's a practical kind of place, where
tying up runner beans is encouraged
where you can water without restriction
where neighbours look out for each other
and Leylandii make good windbreaks.

Interruptions are rare –
just the occasional newcomer
a greeting called out, a hat raised,
news brought from below.

MARILYN RICCI

Momentum

A wild child
runs through the house
pushes over vases
kicks at chairs
up the stairs
into my room where
breathing hard
she jumps on the spot:
I flee! I flee!
then *Wheeeeee!*
down the bannister
out the front door
back over the fields
a receding dot...

Lightning Source UK Ltd.
Milton Keynes UK
UKOW04f1606060116

265929UK00001B/27/P